(HYMN-TUNE)

(...ners who have perished in the mines)

Robert Saint
1936

by the National Union of Mineworkers Gt. Britain.
Saml. Watson, Sec., Durham Area.

(Courtesy NUM Durham Area)

The Durham Miners' Gala

MEMORY LANE

The Durham Miners' Gala

1935-1960

Michael Richardson

breedon **books**
PUBLISHING

First published in Great Britain in 2001 by
The Breedon Books Publishing Company Limited
Breedon House, 3 The Parker Centre, Derby, DE21 4SZ.

ISBN 1 85983 238 5

Printed and bound by Butler & Tanner Ltd, Frome, Somerset
Jacket printing by GreenShires Ltd, Leicester

Contents

Foreword

MEMORY LANE – the Durham Miners' Gala: what an exhilarating title for these photographic recollections of one of the most historic events in the history of the British working class.

The period covered embraces the years from 1935 to 1960, an era when so much changed for the Durham miner and his family.

In the 1930s, the Durham Coalfield was in the midst of depression. Many collieries were laid idle and the miners and their families were facing extreme poverty, a situation compounded by the dreaded 'means test'.

It took the onset of World War Two to create employment again in the Durham collieries. And following the war, the dream of our forefathers – nationalisation – was achieved, thanks to Attlee's Labour government.

Nationalisation meant job security, improved working and safety conditions, and social and economic improvement for the miner and his community.

These Galas celebrated the years of victory and hope, and a better future seemed to be there for the taking. Now the mining communities of Durham were alive and vibrant.

Sadly, the late 1950s and early 1960s witnessed mass pit closures and the compulsory transfer of Durham miners, making them 'industrial gypsies'.

This book captures the miners and their families during 25 years of changing times, through good and bad.

Throughout these years they assembled religiously to attend the 'Big Meeting' and today we still carry on that heritage and history.

This book is a tribute to a great people and their traditions and culture, an invaluable record of the past that will never be forgotten.

I pay tribute to the author, Michael Richardson, for compiling such a fantastic record of our history.

David Hopper
General Secretary
NUM, Durham Area
2001

Introduction

ON 20 November 1869 the first meeting of the Durham Miners' Association was held in the Market Hotel, Durham Market Place. Two years later, on 12 August 1871, 5,000 miners and their families converged upon the city for their first 'Big Meeting'. The venue was Wharton Park, which had been loaned for the occasion by John Lloyd Wharton, MP. The following year it was held on The Racecourse where it has been held ever since, except for the following years: 1915-18, 1921, 1922, 1926 and 1940-45.

This collection brings alive the memories of those who were involved with this special day and enlightens those who never knew it at its peak. This is the first time that so many photographs, showing all aspects of the Gala, have been brought together to cover a specific period. They show the strong community spirit of the people of the Durham coalfield. This comradeship was also evident in times of great sorrow; on 29 May 1951, 83 men lost their lives in the Easington Colliery explosion and the same year an explosion at Eppleton killed nine men. A poignant reminder of the casualties each year was the many banners draped in black.

The 'Big Meeting' was a day of pageantry when the miners entered the city, like the victors of a great battle, with banners held high. In the early 1950s the numbers attending reached an estimated 300,000. Local residents would welcome the opportunity to 'earn a bob or two', Mrs.Jenny Taylor (née Rundle), originally of New Elvet, recalls how she would provide a bowl of clean water and charge 1d for a wash & brush-up. Mrs Margaret Davies, landlady (1937-53) of the Three Hearts of Gold, Church Street, remembers that, the night before, all the interior doors were removed to cater for the crowds.

I am grateful to Mr Frank Bilton, Durham photographer, without whose generosity and wisdom this book would never have been produced. The following two books have been invaluable in the research for this volume: *The Banner Book* by W.A. Moyes (1974) and *Banners of the Durham Coalfield* by Norman Emery (1998).

Michael F. Richardson
2001

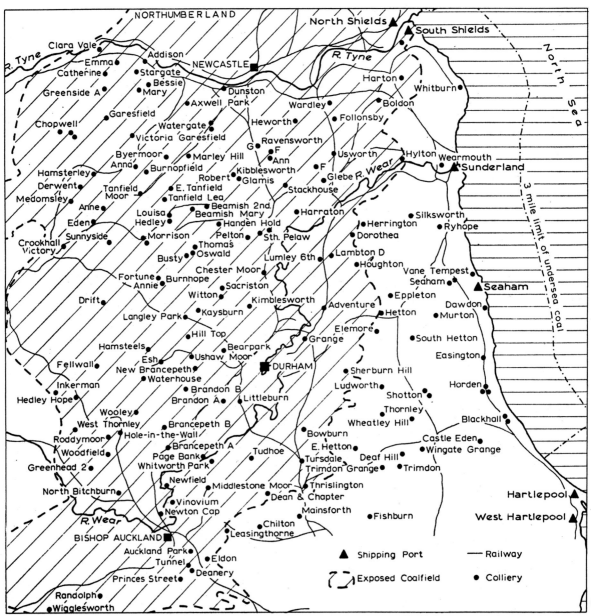

(Courtesy NUM Durham Area)

Durham coalfield showing collieries operating in 1942

Acknowledgements

So many people have donated or loaned photographs to the Gilesgate Archive that it is impossible to thank them all individually. Special thanks go to: Mr Frank Bilton, Mr J. Birch, Mr J. Battong, Mr R. Bowerbank, Mr G. Bowerbank, Mrs W. Coleman, Mr R. Cornwell, the late Donald Crampton, Mr N. Emery, Mr J. Harrop, Mr G. Hales, Mr D. Hopper, Mrs R. Inglis, Mr J. Lawson, Mr C. Lloyd, Mr W. Lough, Mr I.M. McIntyre, Miss D.M. Meade, Mrs G. Neasham, Mr R. Norris, Mr D. Patterson, Mrs N. Richardson, Mr A. Rippon, Mrs A. Robertson, Mr O. Rowland, Mrs M. Shotton, Mr M. Summers and Miss H.C. Webster.

The staff at the following institutions have helped in various ways: Durham City Library, Durham University Library (Palace Green), The Dean and Chapter Library, Darlington Library, Durham Arts, Libraries and Museums Department, The Durham Mining Museum, Breedon Books Publishing Company, Durham Record Office, Beamish Museum, Ward Philipson, The Photo Shop, Carrville, North of England Newspapers, the *Northern Echo*, *Durham Advertiser*, *Evening Chronicle*, *Sunderland Echo*. David Hopper, General Secretary of the NUM, Durham Area, kindly agreed to write the Foreword.

This book is supported by the National Union of Mineworkers, Durham Area, J. & G. Archibald Ltd, builders' merchants, and The City of Durham Trust.

Most of the photographs can be ordered by writing to:
The Photographic Archive
Beamish
The North of England Open Air Museum
County Durham
DH9 0RG

If any readers have new material (ie photographs, slides or negatives) on Durham City and the surrounding area, or any information, the author would be pleased to hear from them. Contact Michael Richardson, 128 Gilesgate, Durham DH1 1QG (0191-3841427).

'Presenting and Preserving the Past for the Future'
The Gilesgate Archive

REMEMBER BEFORE GOD
THE DURHAM MINERS WHO HAVE
GIVEN THEIR LIVES IN THE PITS
OF THIS COUNTY AND THOSE WHO
WORK IN DARKNESS AND DANGER
IN THOSE PITS TODAY

HE BREAKETH OPEN A SHAFT AWAY FROM WHERE MEN SOJOURN
THEY ARE FORGOTTEN OF THE FOOT THAT PASSETH BY. JOB 28.4

The unveiling of the Miners' Memorial in Durham Cathedral, 22 February 1947. The picture includes Tommy Daniels (left) and Harry Inglis (middle) who had been brought from Bearpark Colliery to attend.

Their Big Meeting

I see them invade our fair City with coloured banners high,
I hear the martial music as each Lodge goes marching by;
My heart is filled with Northern Pride that all we miners know,
As I with teeming thousands move, reflect the inner glow.

Oh, come, you Durham Miners, come across the River Wear,
With many a laugh and many a song, and many a hidden tear;
Oh, come, you Durham Miners, come into your own terrain,
For there's a welcome in our hearts you're sure to feel again.

With banners fluttering in the breeze and many a head held high,
Each Lodge comes gaily into view and then goes marching by,
And as they pass the 'County' each band outplays the rest,
For there the Miners' leaders stand with many an honoured guest.

I wonder how these leaders feel as like Generals they view;
The best shock troops of Europe were never quite as true.
They must be proud – Alf Hesler, Charles Pick and all the rest,
To know that passing years have proved they really stood the test.

Above the River Wear, so proud, erect, serene,
The Beautiful Cathedral lends its grandeur to the scene,
As it has done through all the years the miners rallied here,
A monument to all their hopes and to their God so dear.

Long may it stand, thus hallowing the pagentry each year,
And let the Durham Miners come across the River Wear,
And we'll be there, we Durham men, to give a Durham Greeting,
To welcome all the miners as they come to 'THEIR BIG MEETING'.

Mr John McNally
Chairman of the Morrison Busty Lodge

(Courtesy NUM Durham Area)

27 July 1935

Gala speakers
Sir Stafford Cripps MP; Mr Hannen Swaffer; the Rt Hon Herbert Morrison MP and Mr George Lansbury MP.

Cathedral service
Preacher: The Revd Spencer Wade, Rector of Wark-on-Tyne, Newcastle.

Brancepeth Colliery Band, bandmaster J.B. Wright.
Burnhope Colliery Band, bandmaster J. Johnson.
Brandon Colliery Band, bandmaster J. Oliver.

Mayor: Councillor Thomas Plummer.

Historical Notes
25 January
Mr Edward Moore elected agent for the Durham Miners' Association.

16 June
Death of Peter Lee (1864-1935), general secretary of the DMA and chairman of the first Labour-controlled County Council.

8 October
Clement Attlee is elected to succeed George Lansbury as Labour leader.

14 November
General Election. Labour Party in Durham County won all County Divisional seats and also the borough of South Shields.

18 November
Explosion at Dean and Chapter Colliery, one life lost (A. Blood).

North Hetton Colliery, Low Moorsley, ceased production.

Blackhall banner, draped in black, approaches The Racecourse, 1935. The photograph was taken by James Jarché, the accompanying caption reading: 'Revolution looks placid in a bowler hat.'

Spectators in deep thought as they listen to Hannen Swaffer. The attendance this year was estimated between at 150,000 and 200,000.

Mr Hannen Swaffer, the flamboyant journalist. He wrote a report of the Gala for the *Daily Herald*. After the Gala he presented an album of photographs of the day to each of the four speakers. These were taken by James Jarché, one of the leading news photographers of the time.

Sir Stafford Cripps (1889-1952) on the speakers' platform, pausing during his speech. He called upon the miners not to lose sight of their great goal when the workers would control the country, their own lives and their safety. "Until that time is reached," he said, "we must go on fighting ruthlessly against exploitation by capitalism." Largely self-educated, he had helped to found the London Labour Party.

Herbert Morrison (1888-1965), photographed in action on the platform. He was the grandfather of Peter Mandelson, the present MP for Hartlepool and former Northern Ireland Secretary.

Herbert Morrison (left) and Mr Ritson, seated on the speakers' platform taking it all in. Swaffer's caption for this photograph read: "Josh Ritson wonders where he has heard it. Morrison never wonders."

Mr George Lansbury (1859-1940) MP, in full swing. He was a strong supporter of womens' suffrage and defender of conscientious objectors. In 1912 he founded and edited the *Daily Herald*. He was leader of the Labour party (1931-35).

Mr George Lansbury greeting two disabled ex-miners in their pony-driven carts.

Mr George Lansbury accepting a sweet from an admirer.

Spectators in joyful mood on the slopes of The Racecourse. They are all wearing their 'Sunday best'.

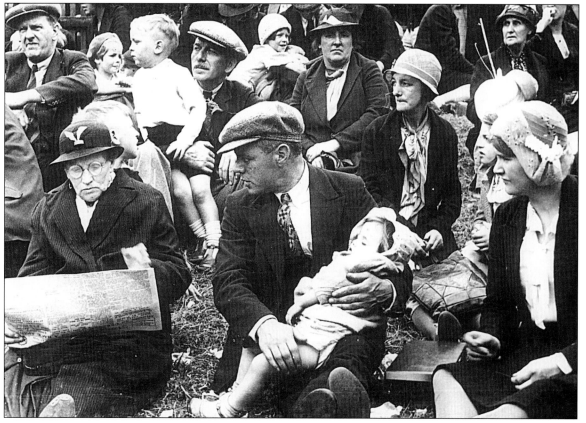

Father is left holding the baby while grandmother reads the newspaper.

The balloon man prepares his wares for a busy day, eyed by a couple of prospective customers. Pelaw Wood can be seen in the distance.

Getting into the swing of things. The showground was a long-established popular attraction at the Gala.

The orderly crowds being directed from The Racecourse by a lone policeman, making their way to the Cathedral for the miners' service. The preacher at the service was the Revd Spencer Wade, himself once a pit-putter at West Auckland Colliery.

Homeward-bound banners make their way up Elvet Bridge towards the Market Place. The mass of people can be seen as far back as Old Elvet.

Blackhall banner makes its way home from The Racecourse. It is draped in black to commemorate a death in the colliery during the past year.

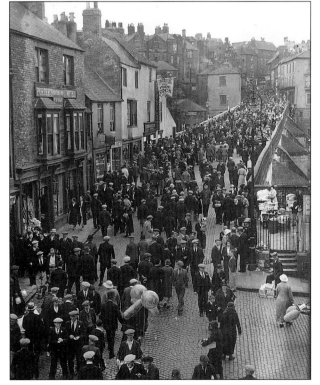

Early afternoon and a quieter scene looking towards Elvet Bridge. On the left is a branch of Porter's, the family grocers, and further to the centre is the 'Rock Shop'.

25 July 1936

Gala speakers
Joseph Jones; the Rt Hon Arthur Greenwood MP;
Mr C.R. Attlee MP and Mr E. Shinwell MP.

Cathedral service
Preacher: The Rt Revd James Geoffrey Gordon, Bishop of Jarrow.

Brancepeth Colliery Band, bandmaster Mr J.B. Wright.
Burnhope Colliery Band, bandmaster Mr J. Johnson.
Brandon Colliery Band, bandmaster Mr J. Oliver.

Mayor: Councillor W.R.H. Gray.

Historical Notes
This year the miners' hymn tune, *Gresford*, was composed by ex-miner Robert Saint. It was dedicated 'to the memory of all miners who have perished in the mines'.

January.
The DMA appointed a full-time solicitor, Mr R.W. Williams, to take charge of compensation and matters of law.

1 July
Mr Sam Watson elected Agent of the DMA.

11 November
The Jarrow Crusade 'snubbed' by the Prime Minister, Stanley Baldwin, who refused to meet the marchers when they arrived in London.

24 November
Explosion at Thornley Colliery, one life lost (R.Waller).
During this year Bishop Middleham and West Thornley collieries ceased production.

Sacriston officials leading their banner up Silver Street. The portraits are those of Robert Smillie (1857-1946), President of the Miners' Federation of Great Britain (left); and Lord Sankey, Chairman of the Coal Industry Commission – his report brought about a shorter working week and increased wages for all colliery workers.

Mr Clement Attlee MP (1883-1967) addresses the crowd from No.2 platform. He had been elected to succeed George Lansbury as Labour leader on 8 October 1935. He openly condemned the means test and said the country needs a strong socialist government that would deal with the causes of poverty and sweep away means test legislation and give to the miners a standard of life based on what the country can afford to all its citizens.

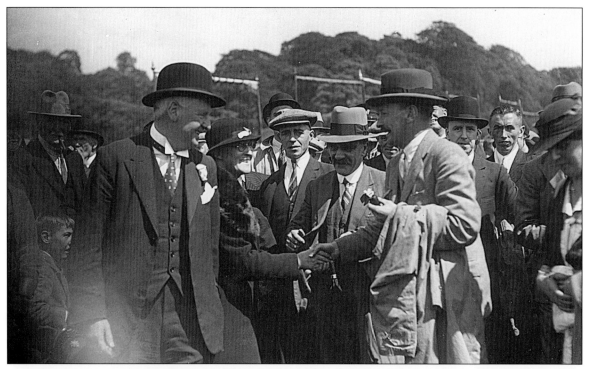

Mr Attlee greets a supporter. The three central figures (left to right) are William Whiteley MP, Mr J.R. Leslie MP, and Mr Attlee. One of the speakers was Mr Shinwell, who had defeated Ramsay MacDonald as member for Seaham in 1935, he said the Gala was 'a wonderful demonstration of working-class solidarity'. This was the fifth time he had spoken at the Gala.

Mr Attlee and Mr Whiteley mingle with the crowd. In his speech Attlee had congratulated the Durham Miner on such a remarkable demonstration of loyalty, which he said was an indication of the desire of the workers for a full life and a determination to get it.

The escapologist is tied up by his assistant. A volunteer bandsman double-checks that the chains are secure. They are watched closely by a spellbound audience. The banner is that of West Stanley.

After the speeches and picnic father takes the children off for some fun.

The bandsmen take the ladies for a trip on the river. One of the attractions of the day was the hire of a boat from Brown's boathouse.

24 July 1937

Gala speakers
The Rt Hon H. Morrison MP; Professor H. Laski; Sir Stafford Cripps MP (and Lady Cripps) and Mr Ebby Edwards.

Cathedral service
Preacher: The Revd R.W. Stannard, Bishop Wearmouth, Sunderland.

Brancepeth Colliery Band, bandmaster Mr J.B. Wright.
Burnhope Colliery Band, bandmaster Mr J. Johnson.
Brandon Colliery Band, bandmaster Mr J. Oliver.

Mayor: Lord Londonderry.

Historical Notes
15 May
One hour reduction from 49 hours per week to 48 hours.

28 May
Neville Chamberlain succeeds Stanley Baldwin as Prime Minister.

19 October
Explosion at Hamsterley Colliery, one life lost.

21 December
Explosion at Murton Colliery, four lives lost (John McKillup, Richard Spry, John Simmons and Thomas Monarch).
There were 10,336 horses and ponies working in the Durham Coalfield this year.

Crowds rest on the slopes of The Racecourse. The attendance this year was around 200,000. Note, top left, the caravans belonging to the showmen.

Mr J.R. Leslie MP, Dr Hugh Dalton MP and Mr W. Whiteley MP (with pipe) photographed beside the platform.

Sir Stafford Cripps MP and Lady Cripps walking among the crowd on The Racecourse. He had spoken on the platform for one hour, warning the miners that collaboration with capitalists might wreck Labour's future.

'All in together!' Bandsmen take a hand in the fun.

The crèche on The Racecourse, a welcome addition for the miners' wives. This was the first time it had been introduced to the Gala. The idea for this was the brainchild of Mrs Hesther Alington, wife of the Dean. She and her friends made themselves responsible for the organisation, which was later taken over by the Mothers' Union.

The family settle down to eat their picnic lunch, making good use of the big bass drum.

'I scream, you scream, we all scream for ice-cream' – this was the caption of the original photograph. Notice the smart attire and the fashionable headgear.

23 July 1938

Gala speakers
George Lansbury MP; Mr C.R. Attlee MP; the Rt
Hon A. Greenwood MP; Mr Joseph Jones; also visitors Mr Alexei Nikolenko, President of the Don-bas miners, USSR, and Dr
Camps, a lady from Spain.

Cathedral service
Preacher: The Very Revd C.A. Alington, Dean of Durham.

Brancepeth Colliery Band, bandmaster Mr J.B. Wright.
Burnhope Colliery Band, bandmaster Mr J. Johnson.
Brandon Colliery Band, bandmaster Mr J. Oliver.

Mayor: Councillor W.E. Bradley.

Historical Notes
16 March
Explosion at Ravensworth Colliery, one life lost.

14 April
Miners' holidays-with-pay agreement to take effect from August.

June
Burnhope Colliery introduced a scheme prohibiting boys under the age of 16 from working underground.

October
A fund was launched by the DMA in support of oppressed Czechoslovakian workers.

November
The DMA Executive Committee forwarded resolutions to the Labour Party, Foreign Secretary and the Prime Minister condemning
the brutal and inhuman treatment meted out by the Nazi Government to the men, women and children of the Jewish race.

Sword dancers outside the Waterloo Hotel, Old Elvet. The building on the left was the County Court offices.

Crowds gather on The Racecourse. The allotments laid out on the other side of the river were worked by the lady students of St Hild's College. A small poster in the centre reads: 'Nuts & Raisins 1d a Bag'.

A trader sells his wares from a cart. The banners (left to right) are those of Sherburn Hill, Sherburn House and Craghead.

Mr Alexei Nikolenko, President of the Don-bas miners (the largest mining district in Russia) talking to Mr Clement Attlee MP on the speakers' platform. The president's speech was relayed to the crowd by an interpreter. He said one of the most important questions was the struggle against Fascism. Germany, Italy and Japan were preparing more terrors against democratic countries. "War may break out at any moment," he said, "and we must spare no strength in trying to avert it through the solidarity of the working class."

A group of miners listening carefully to George Lansbury. In his speech he told the crowd that he wished very much that the President of the French Republic and King George could have stood on the same balcony as "we ourselves and seen the march, representing the real strength and vitality of the Durham Miners".

The Russian miners' leader, Alexei Nikolenko (left) with Mr William Lawther MP. The latter, from Chopwell, had become chairman of the British National Committee of the Friends of Soviet Russia.

The Rt Hon Arthur Greenwood (1880-1954) MP, seated on the slopes of The Racecourse, engages in conversation with a retired miner. Greenwood Aged Miners' Homes, Thornley, were named after him (see Thornley Banner, p138).

A solemn crowd with hats removed listens to the band playing the hymn tune *Gresford* before the speeches begin. This tune was named after the Welsh mining disaster (22 September 1934) when 264 died.

An early afternoon scene on the river bank. Opposite is seen the new concrete retaining wall for Pelaw Wood footpath. In the distance is the old bandstand.

'Stick 'em where you like', was the original caption. Bandsmen try their luck with darts at one of the side-shows. Boxes of chocolates under the dartboards await the lucky contestants.

'Back to back' gave comfort and support to both parties at snack hour.

East Hetton (Kelloe) banner, Kelloe, preparing to leave The Racecourse. On it is the portrait of A.J. Cook with the motto: 'Faithful unto death'. Mr Cook (1883-1931) was a Welsh miner who became secretary of the Miners' Federation of Great Britain.

Crookhall banner on the move towards Old Elvet. Above it, on the skyline, are the old Militia Barracks in Gilesgate.

A banner making its way home along Old Elvet, draped in black.

22 July 1939

Gala speakers
Sir Stafford Cripps MP; Mr Aneurin Bevan MP; Mr Ebby Edwards and the Rt Hon Herbert Morrison MP.

Cathedral service
Preacher: The Very Revd Harry William Blackburn, Dean of Bristol.

Blackhall Colliery Band, bandmaster Mr W. Dawson.
Brandon Colliery Band, bandmaster Mr J. Oliver.
Craghead Colliery Band, bandmaster Mr J. Smith.

Mayor: Councillor W.F. Edge.

Historical Notes
27 April
Conscription begins.

15 May
The Bishop of Durham, Dr A.T.P. Williams, descended the pit shaft of Eppleton Colliery on a three-hour tour of the working underground and on the surface.

3 September.
War with Germany declared.

9 November
Air-raid precautions for collieries introduced.

Mr Ben Wright, aged 75, of Brancepeth, the oldest bandmaster in the county, seen conducting the massed bands in the playing of the miners' hymn tune *Gresford*.

The massed bands playing *Gresford* behind the speakers' platform. The speakers and guests are facing the audience.

Relaxing on the slopes of The Racecourse. Aneurin Bevan MP told the crowds that 'never in history had the working classes of this country exerted less influence in the conduct of public affairs' and 'one result was that thousands were earning less than £2 a week'.

Having a ride on the dodgems. Sir Stafford Cripps had spoken earlier in the day of how the interests of the common people were in danger, due to the present Government. He criticised it for the failure to provide deep bomb-proof shelters for the civilian population; also the failure to store large quantities of food. *Photograph by D.E. Webster of Bede College.*

Blackhall banner showing the portraits of A.J. Cook, Peter Lee and Keir Hardie. The great height of the door easily allows the raised banner to enter. Scenes such as this would have been familiar in medieval times when the craftsmen of the city paraded their banners through the town on Corpus Christi Day in June.

Brandon Colliery banner heads towards the great door of the Cathedral for the miners' service. The preacher was the Dean of Bristol, the Very Revd H.W. Blackburn, who said that it was the most moving service he had ever attended. "To see all those miners, their wives and families, crowded into the cathedral was a scene I shall never forget."

Blackhall Band, conducted by Mr W. Dawson, leaving the cathedral playing Schubert's *Unfinished Symphony*.

Blackhall banner after the service, led by their vicar.

Craghead banner, showing David and Goliath, with the motto: 'He that would be free must strike the first blow.' The band, conducted by Mr J. Smith, had taken part in the playing of voluntaries during the service.

Brandon Colliery banner, bearing a portrait of Thomas Carr and a picture of the west end of the cathedral. The latter had painted over a portrait of Ramsay MacDonald after the miners lost faith in him.

The congregation makes its way towards Palace Green. Note (top) the hat-bearer carrying the head-gear of the bandsmen and the men holding the lodge banner.

The morning after on the fairground, photographed by Mr D.E. Webster.

No Gala was held during World War Two

1940

1 January

Two million men between the ages of 20 and 27 were called up.

May

The Prime Minister, Neville Chamberlain, resigned. Mr Winston Churchill became Prime Minister. He invited members of the Labour Party to join his administration.

June.

The capitulation of France and consequent loss of exports. Many pits were laid idle or were working short-time. The loss of manpower in the Durham coal industry was over 23,000 by end of 1940. Many miners were transferred either to other coalfields or to other work of national importance.

10 June

Italy declared war on the Allies.

November

Dipton Colliery ceased production.

4 December

A massive roof-fall at Sacriston Colliery resulted in the death of five miners (W. Smith, J. Welsh, G.W. Scott, J.W. Britton and W. Richardson).

Easington Colliery pit-sidings were bombed and eight men were killed.

1941

3 March

Compulsory partial pit inspections, following 'Safety in Coal Mines' agreement

17 March

The Government announces plans to conscript women aged 20 and 21 for jobs in industry

20 June

Germany attacks its former ally the Soviet Union

8 December

Britain declares war on Japan.

26 December

Inundation (flooding) at Newfield Drift; one life was lost.
The first competition of the Durham County Brass Band League Championship was held and was won by Blackhall Colliery.

1942

27 February

Explosion at Hetton Colliery; two lives were lost.

17 March

It was announced that coal, gas and electricity were to be rationed.

26 June

Explosion at Murton Colliery; 13 lives were lost (W. Cook, F. Andrews, T.B. Davison, J. Garrett, J. Worth, E.B. Elliott, W. White, A. Lashley, G. Jeffries, G.W. Emery, W. Scott, J. Terry and W.B. Walton).

12 November

Explosion at Eppleton Colliery (R.Coxon).

1942 (continued)
26 December
Explosion at Leasingthorne Colliery; three lives were lost (J. Charlton, H. Dunes [or Dukes] and R. Hunter).

The Durham County Brass Band League Championship was won by Horden Colliery.

1943
27 February
The DMA was affiliated to the National Council of Labour Colleges.

2 December
Ernest Bevin, the Labour Minister, said some conscripts would have to work in the mines and in industry.

The Durham County Brass Band League Championship was won by Crookhall Colliery.

1944
18 January
The first conscripts were sent down the mines and were nicknamed 'Bevin Boys'.

8 March
The miners of South Wales went on strike. 156 collieries out of 200 were laid idle.

23 May
Explosion at Bowburn Colliery; one life was lost (W.D. Gibson).

6 June
D-Day, 18,000 British and American troops landed in Normandy.

24 June
Durham Miners' Rehabilitation Centre for patients suffering from limb injuries was officially opened at The Hermitage, Chester-le-Street.

The Durham County Brass Band League Championship was won by Thornley Colliery.

1945
January.
Formation of the National Union of Mineworkers.

8 May
VE Day. End of hostilities in Europe and unconditional surrender of Germany.

23 May
The wartime Coalition Government resigned.

26 July
General Election: Labour Government elected with clear majority over all other parties.

15 August
The Prime Minister, Clement Attlee, announced the surrender of Japan.

September
Election of Mr J. Kelly as agent of the DMA. Appointment of Mr F. Morris as solicitor.

December.
Election of Messrs J. Foster and J. Joyce as agents of the DMA.

The Durham County Brass Band League Championship was won by Thornley Colliery.

20 July 1946

Gala speakers

The Rt Hon Clement Attlee MP, Prime Minister; the Rt Hon Aneurin Bevan MP, Minister of Health; the Rt Hon Hugh Dalton MP, Chancellor of the Exchequer and Mr Ebby Edwards, Secretary of the NUM.

Cathedral service

Preacher: The Revd J. McManners, Vicar of Ferryhill.

Brancepeth Colliery Band, bandmaster Mr J.B. Wright.
Dean & Chapter Colliery Band, bandmaster Mr W. Graham.
Craghead Colliery Band, bandmaster Mr J. Smith.

Mayor: Councillor J.L. Robson.

Historical Notes

April.
Re-opening of Conishead Priory Convalescent Home, Ulverston, Lancashire.

20 July
First post-war Annual Miners' Gala held.

29 July
Explosion at Addison Colliery; two lives lost (N. Priestey and B. Sweeney)

23 December
Explosion at Ramshaw Colliery, two lives lost (W.A. Hodgson and C. Firby).

There was a shortage of beer at the Gala this year due to strict Government controls by the Ministry of Food.

This year Auckland Park Colliery, Bishop Auckland, ceased production.

The Durham County Brass Band League Championship was won by Hetton Silver Band.

The first post-war Gala seen from Pelaw Wood. Brandon Colliery used this photograph to create its new banner in 1949 (see p87). *Photograph by Charles Hodgson.*

Lambton Colliery banner showing, on the reverse side, Christ walking on the sea, with the motto: 'Oh thou of little faith wherefore didst thou doubt?' The attendance was estimated at around 200,000.

Cornsay banner, followed
by that of Waterhouses,
enters The Racecourse.

The Prime Minister, the Rt Hon Clement Attlee, speaking from No.2 platform. Note the BBC microphone. He said: "I think there is no community in Great Britain more understanding than the men and women of the mining community in Durham. Durham County has not only sent a splendid team of MPs to Westminster but a number of them, hold high rank in the Government."

The audience listen to the Prime Minister. The two tents are those of (left) the ambulance team, and (right) lost children. The *Northern Echo* reported: 'The 62nd Durham Miners Gala will be long remembered, not least because of the well-ordered manner of the great crowd and the fact that for the first time in its history the Prime Minister and four other Ministers of the Crown were present.'

The comedian entertaining the young folk under a banner carrying the motto: 'We seek Knowledge that we may wield power.'

A family band consisting of two piano accordions and a drum-kit strike up a tune for afternoon dancing.

Homeward bound (4.10pm by Bramwell's clock). The great crowd stretches as far as the eye can see. Note the windows boarded-up to prevent people falling through them.

Canopy-top view of the showground.

Craghead banner, the front of which depicts David triumphant over Goliath. The motto reads: 'He that would be free must strike the blow.' The preacher that day was the Revd J. McManners, the first nonconformist to preach at the miners' service.

The Prime Minister, the Rt Hon Clement Attlee, the Rt Hon Aneurin Bevan MP, Minister of Health, the American Ambassador, Mr W. Averell Harriman, the Mayor, Councillor J.L. Robson, civic leaders and guests leaving the Market Place, after a civic reception in the Town Hall. They were walking to the castle where they had dinner, which was provided by Lyons' Café.

Approaching the Castle from Palace Green. Jack Harrison, sword-bearer, leads the dignitaries towards the castle entrance.

26 July 1947

Gala speakers
Rt Hon Ernest Bevin MP, Foreign Secretary;
the Rt Hon Herbert Morrison MP, Lord President of
the Council; Michael Foot MP; Mr A.L. Horner, General Secretary of the NUM.

Cathedral service
Preacher: The Rt Revd Dr Alwyn Williams, The Lord Bishop of Durham.

Brancepeth Colliery Band, bandmaster Mr J.W. Wright.
Dean and Chapter Colliery Band, bandmaster Mr J. Graham.
Thornley Colliery Band, bandmaster Mr E.G.T. Kitto.

Mayor: Councillor H.C. Ferens.

Historical Notes
1 January
'Vesting Day', *ie* Coal industry nationalised. There are 108,291 men employed at 127 Durham collieries.
9 February
Explosion at Derwent Colliery, three lives lost (W. Watson, F. Monaghan and R. Heighway).
22 February
The Miners' Memorial unveiled at Evening Prayer, Durham Cathedral, by The Bishop of Durham.
20 March
Explosion at East Tanfield Colliery, one life lost.
3 July
Watergate Colliery, two lives lost (H. Morgan and W.A. Hopper).
22 August
Explosion at Louisa Old Pit, South Moor, 21 lives lost (H. Talbot, A. Bailey, E. Westgarth, J. Estell, T.M. McKeever, W. Roe, F.E. Martin, T.W. Appleby, J. Rowland, G. Moore, W. Reed, T. Bell (no.1), J.S. Hodgson, T. Bell (no.2), N. Fenwick, J. Chapman, C. Simpson, R.L. Brown, J. Grimley, W. Rutherford and R.W. Birtle).

Four 'sunflowers' are captured by the photographer.

18 September
Inundation (flooding) at Lumley 6th Colliery, two lives lost (G.E. Watson and W. Nelson).
December.
Dunston and Elswick collieries cease production.
The Durham County Brass Band League Championship was won by Shildon London and North Eastern Railway Band.

An early morning scene in the Market Place. Thornley banner is on its way from Claypath to Saddler Street. Note the old police box. Taken by Joseph March.

Late morning (11.45am by Bramwell's clock) and the last banners are seen in the distance, entering Old Elvet. The *Durham County Advertiser* reported that the attendance of 150,000 was, however, less than that of the previous year. Taken by Joseph March.

An afternoon snapshot. The bandsman has exchanged hats with one of his lady companions. His hat carries the initials 'W.H.B.' Possibly Wheatley Hill Band.

Great Expectations. The young man in the centre sports a hat with the motto: 'Kiss me quick'.

'All smile, please, for the camera.' This was the title for the picture which shows a young girl getting in some practice. Many bands welcomed girls as players.

A village mascot, in her homemade costume, prepares to strike up a note. After the war years, a number of banners were led in by such mascots.

A father tells his daughter that she is not too old for a balloon.

Two jolly young couples smile for the camera and fail to attract the attention of the serious men walking by.

Mid-afternoon, relaxing on the riverbank after the picnic lunch.

An old miner, sporting his white muffler and smoking his clay pipe, tells a likely tale to the amusement of the ladies.

A father entertains his young son with a balloon after a tour of the showground.

Three ladies powdering their faces, to the amusement of the photographer. The wording on their fancy bonnets reads (left to right): 'I'm a cuddlesome baby', 'I'll have to ask me mum', and 'What a smasher'.

A young couple take their turn at guarding the instruments. These were the prized possessions of the bandsmen.

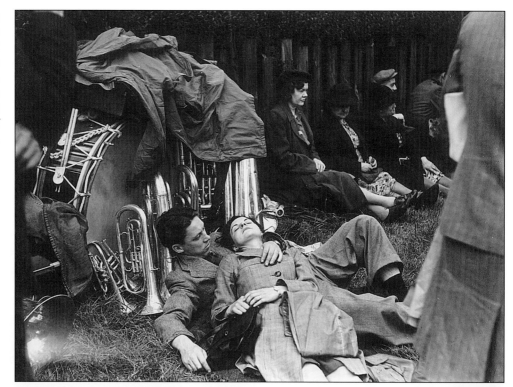

Two miners dance to the delight of the spectators. This was one of the many spontaneous light-hearted performances put on throughout the day.

The smartly-dressed youth of the day from Trimdon Grange congregate in front of their banner. In the centre is Bob Athey.

A plain-clothes band prepares to leave the field for the homeward trek.

The 'Chief Whip' prepares to lead out Mainsforth banner and its cheerful followers.

Hamsteels banner halts for the photographer near the old Neville Hotel (right), North Road, on the journey home. It bears the portraits of Peter Lee and A.J. Cook.

24 July 1948

Gala speakers

The Rt Hon Hartley Shawcross KC, MP, Attorney General; the Rt Hon Sir Stafford Cripps KC, MP, Chancellor of the Exchequer; Rt Hon Aneurin Bevan, MP, Minister of Health; Mr A.L. Horner, General Secretary of the NUM.

Cathedral service

Preacher: The Revd R.A. Beddoes, Vicar of Easington Colliery.

Harton Colliery Band, bandmaster Mr Jack Atherton.

Easington Colliery Band, bandmaster Mr William Delson.

Thornley Colliery Band, bandmaster Mr E.G.T. Kitto.

Mayor: Councillor H.C. Ferens.

Historical Notes

1 April

The electricity industry was nationalised.

April.

Shield Row Drift and the Grange Colliery, Carrville cease production.

June.

Introduction of the NCB Scholarship Scheme.

11 June

Explosion at Sherburn Hill Colliery, four lives lost (F. Hodgson, T.L. Philipson, R. Brown, H. Cowan).

5 July

The introduction of the National Health Service.

October.

Tanfield Moor Colliery ceased production.

December

Gift of the Production Banner to DMA by the firm of Tutill, to be competed for each year.

The Durham County Brass Band League Championship was won by Craghead Colliery.

The Racecourse from Bede College, showing Whinney Hill School in the centre of the skyline. Mr Bevan had said in his speech to the miners that Labour needed 20 years in Government to put Britain back on her feet. Taken by Mr D.E. Webster.

Early morning, and Kimblesworth banner is seen moving across Framwellgate Bridge. Note the old Criterion on the left.

Monkwearmouth banner leaving for home. It portrays a split design showing (1) a miner leaving home to go to work (entitled 'The Last Good Morning'), and (2) his widow seeking aid (entitled 'We Claim Compensation').

Home time, 3.30pm, Elvet Bridge. Usworth banner, showing the portrait of J. Keir Hardie (1856-1915) who was the first Labour MP. He has spoken at the Gala in 1905, 1906 and 1910.

The time is now 3.40pm and looking at this picture it is easy to believe the estimated attendance figure of 250.000, which made it the biggest Gala yet.

At 3.47pm, a band halts at the Magdalen steps and plays a tune, to allow the vast numbers in front of them to proceed. The banner in the distance shows a Biblical scene of Christ walking on the sea.

The homeward-bound miners and their families struggle through Saddler Street towards the Market Place. Many of the onlookers have caught sight of the photographer in his prominent vantage point.

Two mounted policemen clear the way along North Road for the homeward procession. The policeman on the right is Frank Close, of Pittington.

Veronica Hughes and her boyfriend, Thomas Brown, of Elvet, on the showfield. Durham people took advantage of the presence of this attraction on the eve of the Gala, when prices of fairground rides were reduced.

23 July 1949

Gala speakers
The Rt Hon Clement Attlee, CH MP, Prime Minister; the Rt Hon Ernest Bevin MP, Foreign Secretary; the Rt Hon Herbert Morrison MP, Lord President of the Council; Mr Hugh Gaitskell, Minister of Fuel and Power and Mr A.L. Horner, General Secretary of the NUM.

Cathedral service
Preacher: The Rt Revd W.H. Baddeley, The Lord Bishop of Whitby.

Blackhall Colliery Band, bandmaster Mr Harold Laycock.
Thornley Colliery Band, bandmaster Mr E.G.T. Kitto.
Boldon Colliery Band, bandmaster Mr H. Bradley.

Mayor: Councillor J.M. Herring.

Historical Notes
The first competition for the Production Banner was held. It was won by East Tanfield Colliery.

26 April
The National Coal Board (NCB) receives its own coat of arms (see Craghead banner p185).

1 May
The gas industry nationalised.

May 6.
Inundation (flooding) at Thornley Colliery, three lives lost (M. Purvis, W. Rudkin and W. Kelly).

July.
Burnhope Colliery ceased production.

The Durham County Brass Band League Championship was won by Hetton Silver Band.

The Production banner, won by East Tanfield Colliery enters The Racecourse for the first time. It had been made and presented by the firm of Tutils in July 1948. It was competed for annually and awarded to the colliery which had tried the hardest to increase production.

The first banner of the day, that of Mainsforth Colliery, preceded by the officials, makes a dignified entry. It shows the aged miners' homes, Peace Haven, Ferryhill. The gentleman on the right in the light suit is Peter Davies.

South Moor No.1 banner arriving, followed by South Moor No.2.

Mrs Bowie with her husband leads in Chester Moor banner on the occasion of her 50th Gala. The black rosettes attached to the banner signify a death in the pit.

Morpeth Highland pipe band at the head of Washington Glebe miners. The hiring of Scottish pipe bands was due to the shortage of colliery bands. The band leader, a veteran of World War One, proudly wears his medals.

The young men and women follow their banner. Names in the group are Jack Harker, Fred Ryans, Tommy Foster, Ron Liddle, Dorothy Hutchinson, Ronnie Prudhoe, Don Smith, George Harker and George Liddle.

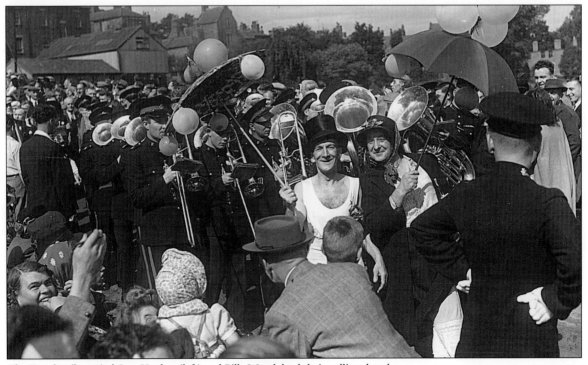

The Dawdon 'beauties', Sam Hughes (left) and Billy Wood, lead their colliery band.

High-spirited young folk compete for attention.

Three young men let off steam to the amusement of the nearby policeman.

One of the speakers, Mr Hugh Gaitskell (1906-1963) Minister of Fuel and Power. He became a socialist during the 1926 General Strike.

Herbert Morrison (right), Mr E. Moore, President of the NUM Durham Area (centre) and Arthur Horner (left), General Secretary of the NUM, on the speakers' platform. Alf Horner had said in his speech that although the miners were critical of some aspects of nationalisation, they would never under any Government go back to the old days of private ownership. The alternative to nationalisation would be economic death.

Brandon's banner seen at its first appearance on The Racecourse. Back row: Mrs Argument, not known, Billy Robinson, Ethel Robinson and Tommy Robinson. Middle row: June Argument, Ivy Lister, not known, Mrs Smith and George Hewitt. Front row: not known, Edith Argument and Norman Robinson. Taken by Ann Robinson.

Sitting proudly in front of Brandon's new banner. Left to right: not known, Derek Argument, Mrs Ann Robinson, Billy Robinson, June Argument (child), Mrs Argument and Mrs Smith.

All the people with Mainsforth banner collect together in front of the speakers platform for a memorable group photograph. The bass drum records the Silver Band's formation in 1909.

23 July 1949

The community of Eden Colliery assembled in front of their banner.

Burnhope Colliery banner. Despite the smiling faces the day was tinged with sadness due the the news of the closing of the colliery. The other banner is that of Houghton Colliery.

Crookhall banner leaving the Market Place into Silver Street. It shows Conishead Priory, the miners' rehabilitation centre which was opened 1930.

A banner, showing the cathedral, attempting to make its way through the Market Place, which is packed to capacity. The *Evening Chronicle* newspaper office is situated behind the banner.

The banner of Crook Drift, known as the 'Hole in the Wall' Colliery, heads towards Silver Street.

The unfurling of Brandon banner by Sam Watson, 9 July. The banner had been designed by Walter Lishman, art master at Durham Johnston School. The scene was taken from a photograph by Charles Hodgson showing the Victory Gala in 1946 from Pelaw Wood (see p54). Taken by Ann Robinson.

22 July 1950

Gala speakers
The Rt Hon Sir Hartley Shawcross KC,
MP, Attorney General; the Rt Hon Aneurin
Bevan MP, Minister of Health; the Rt Hon E.
Shinwell MP, Secretary of State for War; and Mr A.L. Horner, General Secretary of the NUM.

Cathedral service
Preacher: The Rt Revd John Alexander Ramsbotham, Bishop of Jarrow.

Thornley Colliery Band, bandmaster Mr E.G.T. Kitto.
Brancepeth Colliery Band, bandmaster Mr H.M. Hardy.
Lingdale Miners' Colliery Band, bandmaster Mr F. Ramage (with Roddymoor Colliery banner).

Mayor: Councillor Mrs H.H. Rushford (first woman Mayor of Durham).

Historical Notes
February.
Miners' National Fatal Accident Fund Agreement. Re-election of Labour Government.

11 July
Hetton Lyons Colliery, Hetton-le-Hole, ceased production.

July.
Kimblesworth Colliery was Production champion.

19 October
Hugh Gaitskell took over as Chancellor of the Exchequer from Sir Stafford Cripps who was retiring on health grounds.

24 October
Explosion at Etherley Dene Colliery, one life lost (J.E. Wright).

December.
Littleburn Colliery, Langley Moor, ceased production.

The Durham County Brass Band League Championship was won by Craghead Colliery band.

National Association of Colliery Overmen, Deputies and Shotfirers banner at its first unfurling in John Street, Durham City.

Mr R.W. Smith of Sherburn Village (right), who won the competition for the best design, being congratulated by Mr J.G. Sanderson, a former president of NACODS, on the morning of Gala Day. The banner shows a manager, a deputy and a miner clasping hands. Harrison's organ factory is seen on the right.

Two young 'bandsmen' proudly lead in Easington's banner over Elvet Bridge. The fine granite setts, once a feature of Durham's streets, are seen to advantage.

Five smart girls lead their banner over Elvet Bridge. The spire of St Nicholas's Church is visible to the right.

Crowds proceed in leisurely fashion towards Old Elvet. Brown's Boathouse appears in the top right-hand corner.

The last airing of Hetton Lyons Banner. The attached poster explains the reason why.

The 'happy couple' from Dawdon Colliery, Sam Hughes and his 'bride', Billy Wood, with their 'bridesmaid', pause outside the Waterloo Hotel for a wedding snap under the watchful eye of the law. Two of the bandsmen on the right are: John McGrath and Stan Whitwell.

The band leads Lambton banner, draped in black veiling arriving on to The Racecourse. It carries the portrait of A.J. Cook.

Lambton supporters with their banner.

The miners and officials of Leasingthorne Colliery proudly show off their new banner. The showfield is seen in the background.

The arrival of speakers and guests, left to right: Sam Watson, Jack Lawson, the Mayor, Councillor Mrs H. Rushford, Sir Hartley Shawcross and Aneurin Bevan. Mr Bevan spoke of the fear of another world war and said: "We say to Josef Stalin and to communist parties of the world, Let them come once more to the Security Council and ask North Korea to stop fighting."

The Mayor, Councillor Mrs Rushford, receives help with the microphone from Sir Hartley Shawcross. She welcomed the miners and their families, and introduced the speakers.

Crowds in cheerful mood listen to the speakers. Mr Shinwell, Minister for War, described the world as 'crazy' but, referring to the situation in Korea, said: "We must not allow ourselves to be stampeded into action we may ultimately regret."

A family picnic on the racecourse after the speeches. Plastic bags weren't common in those days; everything would be wrapped in newspaper.

Two young bandsmen from Easington Colliery getting in a little extra practice for the return journey (see p96).

'PC 49' on duty on the riverbanks. The *Durham County Advertiser* reported that the Gala had been controlled by 500 policemen, many with walkie-talkie radio sets on their backs.

Two young musicians entertain family and friends.

'Played out and flat out' – mid-afternoon on The Racecourse.

Going home, Bowburn Colliery banner and followers passing the Royal County Hotel. Aneurin Bevan is standing on the balcony bidding them goodbye. Attendance this year was about 200,000.

Trimdon Grange, Women's Section, Labour Party banner turning towards New Elvet, led by Lockwood Band.

Going home, Lambton banner passing the Old Elvet shops.

'Flat out' – the excitement was all too much for this chap. After a few pints of beer he decided to take a nap in a quiet lane off Saddler Street near the Magdalen Steps.

21 July 1951

Gala speakers
The Rt Hon Clement Attlee CH, MP,
Prime Minister; the Rt Hon Herbert
Morrison MP, Foreign Secretary; Mr Michael Foot MP; Mr A.L. Horner, General Secretary of the NUM.
Cathedral service
Preacher: The Rt Revd Douglas Henry Crick, Bishop of Chester.
Easington Public Band, bandmaster Mr C.Peacock (with Elemore Colliery banner).
Brancepeth Colliery Band, bandmaster Mr G. Jacobs.
Wheatley Hill Silver Band, bandmaster Mr W. Forrest (with Wheatley Hill Colliery banner).
Mayor: Councillor J.R.W. Rae.
Historical Notes
April
Durham Miners' Rehabilitation Centre, The Hermitage, taken over by the Ministry of Health.
14 April
Ernest Bevin died, aged 70 years.
May
Arnghyll and Cowley Collieries cease production.
29 May
Explosion at Easington Colliery, 83 lives lost (see p108-9).
6 July
Explosion at Eppleton Colliery, nine lives lost (T. Box, A. Patterson, R. Parkin, J. Walker, A. Hunter, R. Foster and R. Tait; N. Holmes and W.G. Hicks later died of their injuries).
July
Deaf Hill Colliery was Production champion.
December
Introduction of miners' entitlement to two weeks' holiday with pay.
The Durham County Brass Band League Championship was won by Easington Public Band.
The Mayor of Durham's fund this year was for the relief of relatives of the Easington and Eppleton disaster victims.

The grief-stricken faces of Easington Public Band standing in front of the colliery banner in North Road. The bandsman on the far left is Billy Winter, behind the young mascot on the right, is Richard Black. Two other members are Tommy McGarry and Tommy Scott. Less than two months earlier, 83 men (including two rescue-workers) from the colliery lost their lives in an explosion. The pennant hanging from the banner was taken from a wreath which was sent from the miners of Yugoslavia. This is still attached today.

One of the incidents that will long be recalled occurred about one o'clock as the Gala speeches were drawing to a close, and many thousands were clustered round the platforms listening to the Prime Minister on one, and the Foreign Secretary on the other. Away up on the brow of the hill, emerging from Old Elvet, was a lone banner moving slowly over the heads of the vast crowds. No band, no fuss, just a banner like scores of others stationed round The Racecourse. People cheered and clapped hands.

They dashed from every part of the ground as somebody whispered, "Easington…" Yes, it was the banner from the colliery where at the end of May, 81 gallant men were killed in an explosion more than 1,000 feet below the earth's surface. The banner was draped in black and below the portraits of Bob Smillie and Keir Hardie was the name of the colliery and above a representation of the pithead. On the other side is a picture of Easington's Welfare Hall. This banner became synosure of every eye as it was borne aloft by solemn-faced and perspiring miners to its stand near the riverside. Men and women fondled the cloth as though they were trying to shake hands with the men who gave their lives. They looked at the portraits and the picture as though they had never seen a banner before, but there was a special reason for this attention: it was Easington's banner.

We had thought it was arranged that this should be the last banner to arrive, and that it should come without the music of a band. But that was not so. "We have a band," said an officer of the miners' lodge, "but we left them in Elvet."

"Why are you last in the procession?"

"Because we were held up at some points along the route and could not get here before the speeches."

We saw, too, the Eppleton banner and its tragic reminder of that other explosion where seven noble miners lost their lives…

Durham County Advertiser (27 July 1951)

A memorial photograph of Eppleton (6 July) and Easington (29 May) disaster victims. The nine Eppleton men appear along the bottom of the picture. *Reproduced by kind permission of The Durham Mining Museum.*

IN MEMORIAM

JOHN ANSON
WILLIAM ARMSTRONG
MARK SMART BEDDING
MATTHEW BLEVINS
GEORGE BRENKLEY
THOMAS BRENKLEY
LOUIS BRENNAN
GEORGE MILLER BROWN
HENRY BURDESS
BERTRAM BURN
EMMERSON CAIN
FREDERICK CAIRNS
GEORGE CALVERT
JAMES CALVIN
FREDERICK CARR
GEORGE WILLIAM CARR
JAMES CARR
JOHN EDWIN CHALLONER
RICHARD CHAMPLEY
JOSEPH CHARLTON
ALBERT KERR CHAPMAN
JOHN CLOUGH
WILLIAM ARTHUR DRYDEN
JOHN ELLISON
CHARLES FISHBURN
HENRY FISHBURN
THOMAS GARSIDE
JOSEPH GODSMAN
ALBERT GOWLAND
GEORGE GOULBURN
ERNEST GOYNS
HERBERT GOYNS
JOHN HARKER
JOHN WILLIAM HENDERSON
THOMAS HEPPLE
DANIEL HUNT
STEPHEN HUNT
WILLIAM HUNT
ARTHUR CHAMBERS HUTTON
FREDERICK ERNEST JEPSON
HERBERT JEFFREY JOBLING
LAWRENCE JONES

THOMAS EDWARD JONES
JOHN KELLY
WILLIAM KELLY
JOHN EDWARD ARMSTRONG LAMB
JESSE STEPHENSON LINK
JOSEPH FAIRLESS LIPPEATT
PETER LYNCH
DENIS McROY
WILLIAM JAMES McROY
ROBERT WILLIAM MILBURN
HAROLD NELSON
ALBERT NEWCOMBE
NORMAN NICHOLSON
ROBERT NOBLE
WILLIAM EDWARD FORBES PARKS
WILLIAM PARKIN
ROBERT PASE
STANLEY PEACEFUL
ALEXANDER PENMAN
JAMES PORTER
JOHN THOMAS PORTER
THOMAS VALENTINE RICE
JOHN ROBINSON
JOHN GEORGE ROBSON
GEORGE SCOTT
ALBERT SEYMOUR
FREDERICK SILLITO
GEORGE HENRY STUBBS
MATTHEW WHITE SURTEES
HUGH BELL SURTEES
LAURENCE THOMPSON
THOMAS THOMPSON
THOMAS TRISNAN
ROBERT TURNBULL
JACK YOUNG WALLACE
GEORGE WILKIE
REGINALD WILKINSON
MATTHEW WILLIAMS
ROBERT WILLINS
JOHN WILSON
STEPHEN WILSON

Easington victims.

IN MEMORIAM

T. BOX
R. FOSTER
W.G. HICKS
N. HOLMES
A. HUNTER
R. PARKIN
A. PATTERSON
R. TAIT
J. WALKER

Eppleton victims.

Mr Attlee and Herbert Morrison welcome the banners from the balcony of the Royal County Hotel. The Gala attendance was the largest in its history with over 300,000 people packing the streets of Durham.

Villages from East Hetton (Kelloe), in joyful mood, follow their banner as it makes its way through Old Elvet.

The new Bearpark banner makes its first Gala appearance, Old Elvet. The banner shows Bearpark Aged Miners' Homes. Names of some people on the photograph are left to right: William McLoughlin, Robert Oliver, Benny Blake, Jonty Turnbull, Jimmy Leng, Freddy Crooks, Barry Crooks, Sammy Crooks, Jack Cutty, John R. Cummings, William Greenwell, Robert Shotton, Danny Mullin.

Randolph Lodge, Evenwood banner, depicting a view of the colliery coke-yard and railtrack. The smaller banner, that of Lumley, portrays four blacksmiths at an anvil, beating swords into ploughshares.

The village 'Mr Universe', Lawrence Dutton of Easington Lane, leads in Elemore banner to the amusement of the crowds.

The speakers leave from the rear of The Royal County Hotel for the platform on The Racecourse, escorted by Chief Constable Alex Muir. Front: Herbert Morrison, Mr and Mrs Attlee, and Sam Watson.

A welcome cheer from the crowds as the Prime Minister nears the platform.

The prime minister addressing the crowds from the platform. He first expressed his sympathy with the bereaved families, of the Easington and Eppleton disasters. He said: "I never forget the continual toll that goes on in the mines, and I know that my colleagues, immediately concerned with these affairs, are consistently working to reduce the toll." Seated at the table are Arthur Horner, Sam Watson and the Mayor, Councillor Rae.

Speakers seated on No.2 platform are Herbert Morrison, Mr E. Moore and Michael Foot.

Herbert Morrison, the Foreign Secretary, swings into action.

Michael Foot, MP for the Devonport Division of Plymouth, makes his first Gala speech. He spoke of social revolution provoked by world poverty: "We should welcome the chance to shape and guide it properly and to offer …an honourable partnership in the building of the world."

Mr Arthur Horner (1894-1968), who was president of the South Wales miners from 1936-46 and General Secretary of the N.U.M. from 1946-1959. In his speech he reminded those who only remember the miner when great disasters occur, that 700 had died the previous year (1950) from silicosis (a lung disease).

Father lifts up the girls for a photograph outside Lloyds Bank in the Market Place.

Relaxing on the banks of the Wear under the majestic Durham skyline. The spire of St Nicholas's Church is seen on the right; a memorial service was held there for those who died in the Easington and Eppleton disasters.

The 5th Seaham Boy Scouts band drums up a beat for the pleasure of its followers and the surprise of the young chap on the base drum. The base drummer is Bill Dyson and behind him is Freddy Welsh, both from Seaham.

Vane Tempest band and banner leaving for the homeward trek. Sherburn Hill banner (on the left) is still attached to the railings.

Mr Attlee, Sam Watson and (far left), Mr E. Moore, wave the miners goodbye from a window in the Royal County Hotel. The little girl is Sam Watson's daughter, Christine.

The unfurling of East Hetton banner on the eve of the Gala at Kelloe by Mr Attlee, whose portrait it carried. Mrs Attlee is seated to the left. Note the pit heap to the left of the picture.

The unfurling of Bearpark banner on the eve of the Gala. It shows the Bearpark Aged Miners' Homes. Alderman W. Kingston performed the unveiling. He had held the record in the village for leading in the banner for over 50 years.

26 July 1952

Gala speakers
The Rt Hon Aneurin Bevan MP; the Rt Hon Sir Hartley
Shawcross, QC MP; Miss Margaret Herbison MP and Mr A.L. Horner, General Secretary of the NUM.

Cathedral service
Preacher: Dr Alan Richardson, Canon of the Cathedral.

Thornley Colliery Band, bandmaster Mr E.G.T. Kitto (with Washington 'F' banner).
South Moor Colliery Welfare band, bandmaster Mr Robert Allan (with joint Lodges South Moor Group banner).
West Pelton and Beamish Collieries Band, bandmaster Mr A. McLean Snr (with the Beamish Mary banner).

Mayor: Councillor G. McIntyre.

Historical Notes
22 April
Death of Sir Stafford Cripps, former Labour Chancellor of the Exchequer.

July
Heworth Colliery was Production champion.

3 October
Britain explodes its first, atomic bomb on the Monte Bello Island, North West Australia.

11 November
Herbert Morrison defeats Aneurin Bevan for the deputy-leadership of the Labour Party.

December.
Death of Mr J. Gilliland, former president of DMA.

The Durham County Brass Band League Championship was won by Crookhall Colliery.

Blackhall banner coming down North Road, bearing the portraits of A.J. Cook, Peter Lee and Keir Hardie. The old Station Hotel (demolished in the 1960s) is seen on the right.

Crowds passing the old bus station, North Road. On the right is the Vaudeville café and to the left Metcalfes' chemist shop.

A line of young merry-makers from Ushaw Moor captures the mood of the day.

The same youngsters dancing their way further along the street, lead Waterhouses banner. The Dunelm Hotel, to the right of the banner, is now part of the Royal County Hotel.

Dawdons' new banner and followers outside the Royal County Hotel, preceded by three mascots (Sam Hughes, not known, and Billy Wood). The banner shows a woman at a table teaching a child, with the motto: 'Knowledge is Power.'

Among the group on the balcony this year was the Very Revd J.H.S. Wild, Dean of Durham, who had accepted the invitation of the DMA to join it. The banner passing by bears the portrait of James Keir Hardie.

Aneurin Bevan (1897-1960) recognises a friend (on the right is Hugh Dalton). Bevan was one of 13 children and he began work in the South-East Wales coalfield at the age of 13. In the 1926 General Strike, he led the Welsh miners.

An orderly procession following Crookhall banner. A proud young girl takes her place in front of the band. In the distance is the banner of Beamish Air Colliery.

Crowds on The Racecourse, showing on the opposite side of the river the teacher training colleges of Bede (left) and St Hild's (right).

Speakers walking towards the racecourse. Front (left to right): Sam Watson, Aneurin Bevan, the Mayor, Councillor G. McIntyre and Margaret Herbison. Rear, on the left: Mr D.B. Martin Jones and the Mayoress, Mrs M.J. McIntyre.

Mr Sam Watson, secretary of the DMA, cracks a joke in his introduction of Mr Bevan, to the amusement of those behind him.

Bevan greets the crowd, He said: "When I was watching the banners come in, I saw A.J. Cook's portrait, side by side with that of Peter Lee; and I remembered how they used to quarrel like 'Kilkenny cats'. Now they are no longer quarrelling. Why? Because they are dead."

Mr Bevan receives water from Margaret Herbison, after his 50-minute address.

Margaret Herbison was only the fifth woman to be invited to speak in the history of the Gala. She said she was delighted to see the strength of solidarity among the men and women of the Durham coalfield.

Mr Sam Watson (1898-1967) feeling the heat at 1pm. He was born at Donkin's Row, Boldon Colliery. At the age of 14 he started working in the mines. His first official post was secretary of Boldon Independent Labour Party in 1927; in 1936 he became agent for the DMA. He was awarded the CBE in 1946 and an honorary degree by the University of Durham in 1955. He was known to many as 'Mr Big Meeting' for the work he did in promoting the Gala.

Mr A.L. Horner, General Secretary of the NUM, platform No.2. He told the miners that the Tory Government must not ignore their request for a minimum weekly wage of £8 10s underground and £7 10s on the surface. At that time they were receiving £7 1s 6d and £6 0s 6d, respectively. (Mr E. Moore is seated at the table.)

Sir Hartley Shawcross, platform No.2. He said that everybody, not least 'the mean, muddled and mischievous men gathered together in Mr Churchill's administration, knew that Labour would go back to full power at the next election'.

The vast audience swelters under the midday sun during the speeches.

Speakers and guests leave The Racecourse for lunch at the Royal County Hotel.

Light refreshments, ice-cream soda and cola.

The parents concentrate on what the speaker has to say, while the young lad quenches his thirst.

Father entertains
the children after
the speeches.

'Time for a nap.'
For some, the
excitement and
fine weather was
too much.

A grandfather treats his grandchildren to ice-cream and a toffee apple from the fairground.

Fun-time for the younger ones on the fairground rides.

Miners and friends cool their thirst outside the Half Moon Hotel, bottom of New Elvet.

Open-air drinking in the yard of a city public house. Casualty figures were low this year. The County Hospital had one patient who had drunk too much. Dryburn admitted one client who was suffering from minor injuries due to a brawl.

East Hetton banner, showing the portrait of Mr Attlee, leaving The Racecourse for home.

Esh Winning leads the outgoing banners home followed by that of Sherburn Hill.

Despite the antics of their 'leader' the people escorting South Hetton banner make a dignified progress up Claypath, with the afternoon sun behind them. The doorway on the right now leads to Durham City Labour Club.

Bandsmen pause in front of Bramwell's the optician on Elvet Bridge. The two who are minus their jackets and hats give an indication of the glorious weather that year.

18 July 1953

Gala speakers
The Rt Hon Clement Attlee CH, MP; the Rt Hon
Herbert Morrison MP; Mrs Barbara Castle MP; Sir William Lawther and Mr A.L. Horner, General Secretary of the NUM.

Cathedral service
Preacher: Dr J.L.Wilson, Dean of Manchester (former curate in charge at St John's, Neville's Cross).
Thornley Colliery Band, bandmaster Mr E.G.T. Kitto.
Craghead Colliery Band, bandmaster Mr E.W. Cunningham.
Mainsforth Colliery Band, bandmaster Mr R.L. Smith.

Mayor: Councillor J.R. Kingston.

Historical Notes
March.
Blaydon Burn (Mary) Colliery ceased production.

23 March
Explosion at Horden Colliery, one life lost (Joseph H. Blackburn).

July.
New Brancepeth Colliery ceased production.

July.
South Pelaw Colliery was Production champion.

October.
Commencement of work on the Memorial Garden at the Miners' Hall, Red Hill, Durham.

The Durham County Brass Band League Championship was won by Crookhall Colliery Band.

New Brancepeth banner coming down North Road for the last time because the colliery ceased production this month. All the buildings in the picture were demolished in the 1960s for the new road scheme which linked Millburngate Bridge to North Road. The railway viaduct is visible at the top of the picture. Taken by Mrs G. Neasham.

Dancers a little further along the street, passing the Dunelm Hotel (see opposite page).

Mr Attlee and friends watch the dancers from the balcony. Many miners threw matchboxes up to the speakers to have them autographed. Barbara Castle is in the centre, wearing the light coloured dress.

Marsden banner, bearing the picture of the famous rock. The building behind was later demolished and in its place was built the Catholic Chaplaincy, Old Elvet. Taken by Chris Crawford.

Thornley's new banner makes it first public appearance on The Racecourse. Names of the men are: G. Soppit, J. Morland, J. Joicey, J. Robson, M. Kirk, D. Swallow, E. Carter, J. Webb, J. Williams, W. Dowden, D. Gott, J. Cherry, S. Greener, L. Wilkinson and W. Cowan.

Happy-go-lucky youngsters from East Hetton (Kelloe) on The Racecourse. Faces identified are: Tones, Billy Wilkinson, Arnold.

Mr E. Moore, Sir William Lawther and Councillor J.C. Robson, NUM officials in the courtyard of the County Hotel. Lawther in his speech said: "Today Labour is at the crossroads. Beware of those who sling catchphrases and spin words to suit the times. Avoid them as you would the plague."

The banners of South Moor No.1 (right) and No.2 (left). No.1 depicts the aged miners' homes; No.2 shows a fallen miner being raised by the Angel of Faith, with the figure of Justice standing close by. After taking the weight off his shoulders the bass drummer stretches out in front of his fellow bandsmen.

The spectators listen attentively at No.2 platform. On the skyline, right-hand side, flies the police pennant of the mobile unit.

Mr E. Moore, president of the NUM Durham Area, makes his last official appearance on No.2 platform before his retirement. He expressed concern at low output of coal. He said that, since 1947, the Durham coal trade had made a profit for only one month. He urged miners' lodges to give earnest consideration to these matters. (Barbara Castle is seated on the left.)

Party-time on The Racecourse. Mrs Dorothy Peel of Trimdon, was one of the star dancers at the Gala, performs for a mainly youthful audience.

Sherburn Hill's new banner on The Racecourse, showing the aged miners' homes. The strong, vibrant presence of young faces is evident among the 'clan'.

The miners and families of South Pelaw Colliery pose as the victors, having been awarded the Production banner for their hard effort during the year.

The people of Eden and Derwent collieries share a photograph before their banners (Eden: central sick-bed; Derwent: David triumphing over Goliath).

The Horden comrades with their banner which shows the portraits of A.J. Cook, Peter Lee and Robert Smillie. On the right is the conspicuous figure of the only woman member of the band.

17 July 1954

Gala speakers

The Rt Hon Sir Hartley Shawcross, QC MP; the Rt Hon Aneurin Bevan MP; Mrs Bessie Braddock MP and Mr A.L. Horner, General Secretary of the NUM.

Cathedral service

Preacher: The Most Revd Dr Cyril Garbett, Lord Archbishop of York.

Crookhall Colliery Band, bandmaster Mr Jack Stobbs.
Silksworth Colliery Band, bandmaster Mr J. Peacock.
Langley Park Colliery Band, bandmaster Mr G. Dover.

Mayor: Councillor Mrs E. Blyth.

Historical Notes

January
Mr C. Pick elected agent for DNA.

May
Official opening of Easington Colliery Memorial and Garden of Remembrance.

July
Follonsby (Wardley) Colliery was Production champion.

17 July
For the first time no trains operated from Elvet Station on Gala day.

August
Axwell Park Colliery ceased production.

At Fishburn a new £2 million Coke Oven Plant was opened, employing about 180 men. Opening of Metal Bridge Drift Mine by the NCB at Ferryhill.

The Durham County Brass Band League Championship was won by Crookhall Colliery.

Byermoor banner coming over Elvet Bridge. The banner shows a picture of Mr Attlee set above the Houses of Parliament, with the motto: 'Organisation the key to economic freedom.'

Chester Moor banner outside the Waterloo Hotel, Old Elvet, showing The Hermitage, Chester-le-Street. On the right is the author's uncle, Paddy McManus, with his son Peter on his shoulders.

The new banner of Crookhall Colliery, making it first appearance at the Gala, resting outside the Royal County Hotel. It was designed by Frank Burden, a local man, and shows a modern miner surrounded by illustrations connected with the Durham Coalfield.

Speakers and guests on the Royal County Hotel balcony; Bessie Braddock, Aneurin Bevan and Sir Hartley Shawcross are among them.

Mrs Lilian Crampton and her son Donald outside their shop in New Elvet. Gala day was an ideal opportunity to expand business. Donald later ran the shop until his retirement.

Young people from Bowburn ahead of their banner. Names include Jack Ord, Jacky Downs and Joyce Whyley. The boys are wearing their girlfriends' coats over their own.

A 'young' dancer gets support from the conductor as she prepares to lead Ushaw Moor banner. The bag-carrier on the right breaks out into a fit of laughter.

Dancing in with the banner.

The 'bride' (Billy Wood) and 'groom' (Sam Hughes) with the 'best man' at the head of Old Elvet lead in the Dawdon banner.

Miners' Day from The Gables, St Hild's Lane. Painted by Durham City artist, Hilary C. Webster, aged 14, this painting won a BBC Radio *Children's Hour* competition in 1954.

Crowds on the slopes of The Racecourse smile for the camera. Behind them are the caravans belonging to the showmen.

The youth connected with Washington 'F' Pit step out eagerly in front of their banner which shows the cathedral.

Seated crowds on the 'slope'. Shortly before the speeches began, a serious incident occurred. A woman from Ferryhill, who was with her husband, collapsed after being shot by an air rifle. The shot was believed to have come from Pelaw Wood, but the culprit was never caught.

The large contingent with Mainsforth banner advances on to The Racecourse. The reverse side of the banner shows the picture of Conishead Priory.

Easington banner, draped in black, displaying the portraits of Keir Hardie and Robert Smillie.

The speakers near the swimming baths on their way to The Racecourse; Bessie Braddock, Sam Watson and his daughter Christine, Aneurin Bevan, Sir Hartley Shawcross and the Mayor, Councillor Mrs E. Blyth.

The crowd listens intently to the speakers. Mrs Braddock told the miners that it had been reported that she was a rebel. She agreed that she was a rebel and if there was any trouble with the workers, she would be with them.

Usworth banner, showing the portrait of Keir Hardie, was the first to pass through the Market Place at 8.05am. Their mascot, a miner dressed as Old Mother Riley, takes centre-place.

The community of Crookhall and its banner approaches the Cathedral.

Langley Park banner enters Palace Green for the cathedral service. The banner shows an ideal scene with newly-built houses and pleasant gardens in a tree-lined street entitled, 'Our Aim'. The Archbishop of York, Dr C. Garbett said that one reason he had wanted to attend the Gala was to thank the miners for all they had been doing for the country. 'I know your work is carried on in darkness and often in danger and we should therefore be all the more grateful for what you have done.'

Silksworth banner and band, led by their priest, make a dignified procession to the cathedral.

Black-and-white minstrels
accompany Blackhall banner.

Blackhall banner on The Racecourse showing the portrait of A.J. Cook. Left to right: not known, Mr Arthur Wilkinson, husband of Arthur Cook's daughter, who is in the centre; Mr Arthur Horner is holding their son.

Horden Labour and Trade Union banner showing the motto: 'He who laughs most works hardest', approaches Elvet Bridge, led by a grinning 'Stan Laurel' character.

16 July 1955

Gala speakers
The Rt Hon Clement Attlee OM, CH, MP; the
Rt Hon Hugh Gaitskell MP; Mr Michael Foot and Mr A.L.
Horner, General Secretary of the NUM.

Cathedral service
Preacher: The Rt Revd A.M. Ramsey, Lord Bishop of Durham.
Crookhall Colliery Band, bandmaster Mr J.J. Stobbs.
Easington Public Band, bandmaster Mr C. Peacock (with Elemore Colliery banner)
Handen Hold Colliery Band, bandmaster Mr A. McLean.

Mayor: Councillor H.L. Cawood.

Historical Notes

January
Causey Mill Drift ceased production.

26 May
General Election. Conservative Government re-elected
with Sir Anthony Eden as Prime Minister.

June
Mr Sam Watson received an Honorary Degree of Doctor of
Civil Law from Durham University.

July
Tudhoe Park Colliery was Production champion.

16 July
Visit of a Russian delegation to the Gala.

August
Rose Cottage Drift ceased production.

September
Quarry Drift and Etherley Dene Colliery (both near Bishop
Auckland) ceased production.

14 December
Hugh Gaitskell was elected Labour Party leader.
The Durham Brass Band League Championship was won
by Crookhall Colliery.

Shotton banner, showing Conishead Priory, arrives from New Elvet. At the rear of the procession extra police reinforcements are arriving for duty (400 were drafted). The buildings in the centre, to the left of the garage, were later demolished and are now replaced by university lecture rooms.

A general view of The Racecourse from Pelaw Wood. The skyline is dominated by the majestic Norman cathedral.

16 July 1955

The Chief Constable, Alex Muir, leads Mr Attlee and his wife towards the platform, meeting en route an impassable crowd. The 'Mounties' soon altered that by gently nudging a way through.

The Mayor, Councillor H.L. Cawood, gives a civic welcome as Sam Watson looks on. Councillor Cawood mentioned that his grandfather, Benjamin Cawood, was a lay missioner in Durham in the year that the first Gala was held in 1871.

At least 13 ice-cream vans are lined up along the riverside footpath doing a roaring trade. Durham University Observatory had reported a temperature of 78 degrees Fahrenheit.

The Russian delegation at the Gala. On the far right is Ivan Rossochinsky, President of the Central Committee of the Russian Mine-Workers' Union. The names of the other three delegates are Alexi Korshunov (a face-worker), Nikolai R. Serbinovich (a combine-operator) and G.Kuznetson (interpreter).

Ivan Rossochinsky presents a banneret to Sam Watson, who receives it on behalf of the Durham Miners. It carried greetings in English on one side, and in Russian on the other. On the left is the Mayor, Councillor Cawood, and Hugh Gaitskell.

Young autograph hunters press forward eagerly to collect the Russian leader's signature.

Mr Ken Ramshaw, the youngest member of the Durham Miners' Executive, a check-weighman of Handen Hold Lodge, proposes a vote of thanks to the speakers. Clement Attlee MP is seated far left.

The massed gathering basks in the midday sun listening to the speakers. The *Durham County Advertiser* reported that the estimated attendance was less than that of the previous year, which had been 200,000. It is difficult to believe this when looking at these photographs.

Guests on the platform, keeping cool in the afternoon sun when temperatures reached over 80 degrees Fahrenheit. Mrs Attlee is seated on the right.

A mounted escort precedes the chief constable, who is followed by Mr Attlee and his wife, from The Racecourse towards the Royal County Hotel.

Families cooling their feet at Bede College boat-landing.

The entertainer with his banjo finds a quiet corner to make music. The public houses did a roaring trade as they where allowed to stay open for 12 hours.

Dancing on the showfield. Earlier in the day, the Chief Constable, Alex Muir, was taken for an impromptu dance. One of the young dancers in front of a banner seized the end of his walking stick and dragged him into the throng. Mr Muir kept a firm hold until, smiling, he was released.

Girls resting on the slopes.

A work of art with plastic cups which had been discarded by the thirsty thousands. One stall at the fairground gave visitors a surprise – the commodity it offered was water, and the price was one penny a cup.

A St John Ambulance man to the rescue of a young glass victim. A record number of 300 cases was dealt with by these men and also by members of the Nursing Division on The Racecourse alone. Broken glass and exhaustion due to the heat were the main cases.

New Herringtons' old banner going home for the last time, as it was replaced by a new one the following year.

The unfurling of Ushaw Moor banner on the eve of the Gala by Mrs Attlee, showing the portrait of Jack Joyce. He had spent his working life at Ushaw Moor Colliery where he served his fellow miners as check-weighman and compensation secretary. In January 1946 he was elected financial secretary of the DMA.

21 July 1956

Gala speakers
Mr R.H.S. Crossman MP; Mr L.J.
Callaghan MP; Mr R.W. Williams MP and Mr
A.L. Horner, General Secretary of the NUM.

Cathedral service
Preacher: The Rt Revd Noel Baring Hudson, Lord Bishop of Newcastle.

Horden Colliery Band, bandmaster Mr J.D. Scoines.
Craghead Colliery Band, bandmaster Mr E.W. Cunningham.
Eden Colliery Welfare Band, bandmaster Mr A. James.

Mayor: Councillor J.R. Thurlow.

Historical Notes
July
Opening of Tursdale Training and Education Centre.

July
South Hetton Colliery was Production champion.

27 July-17 August
NUM, Durham Area, miners' delegation visited USSR as guests of the Central Committee of Russian Mineworkers.

16 October
Bildershaw Colliery (near West Auckland) ceased production.

November
Blaydon Burn Bessie Pit ceased production.
The Durham County Brass Band League Championship was won by Crookhall Colliery.

Blackhall gypsy mascots bringing in their band, banner and followers past Staddon's toy shop, North Road (see p178). A Scottish pipe band, Old Elvet, lead Monkwearmouth banner.

A Scottish pipe band, Old Elvet, lead Monkwearmouth banner.

A young trainee
trombonist marches with
the band. The bandmaster
has the letters 'H.C.B.' on
his hat.

Two lines of lads (with one girl) wave their way up Old Elvet. One of the spectators at the window of the Dunelm Hotel looks dangerously close to falling out.

Girls wearing the bandsmen's hats lead Wooley banner. The banner shows a miner, cap in hand, offering support to a weeping widow with her three children at a graveside.

Rock 'n' Roll to the Gala. High spirits in Elvet when these two girls get under way with the new dance craze.

One of the lads is swept off his feet by his marras.

The male part of this trio arrived at The Racecourse minus his shirt after a 'hot dance' session through the city. East Hetton (Kelloe) banner is behind them.

The arrival of Blackhall Gypsy Troupe.

Young folk swaying on to The Racecourse ahead of a colliery band.

The most sought-after position on The Racecourse was 'the Slopes'. From there all the processions could be seen to their best advantage.

Evenwood band's big bass drummer, Mowbray Maughan.

'Davey Crockett', alias George Cairns, from Bowburn Colliery, one of the banner carriers. Thanks to the film starring Fess Parker, this year coon-skin hats and tails were to be seen everywhere. About a dozen 'Mr Crocketts' entered a Church Street hostelry, only to be met with howls of derision and laughter. Out fled the 'heroes', their pride injured and one minus his tail.

The Mayor, Councillor Jack Thurlow, next to Lord Attlee who is followed by Countess Attlee and Mr S. Watson make their way towards the platform. Sam Watson paid tribute to the Attlees for the great work they had done for the Labour movement. Referring to the recently conferred Earldom Mr Watson said: "To Durham miners they will always remain Clem and Vi."

Nearing the platform, the Mayor, Jack Thurlow of Gilesgate, spots the photographer. The banners on the right are from Trimdon Grange and Silksworth.

Customers from the
Court Inn, outside the
Police Headquarters in
Court Lane.

Mr R.H.S. Crossman, speaking from No.2 platform, makes a point. Mr R.W. Williams, far left (at the table), was the Durham miners' solicitor from 1936-45; second left is Mr J. Kelly, the Durham miners' president; and third left is Mr E. Moore.

Youngsters display their glove-puppets, trophies from the fairground.

Horden band, playing *Sanctuary of the Heart*, as it slowly and reverently approaches the cathedral. Among the bandsmen are the Craddocks, father and son (both named William), also Harry and Albert Hirst.

Craghead Colliery officials proceed towards the cathedral with their banner, which shows the NCB coat-of-arms and the motto: 'Independence, Liberty and co-operation.'

With the fine back-drop of Cosin's Hall and the medieval almshouses, the Revd W. Portsmouth leads Eden banner and band across Palace Green for the miners' service. Bill and Melvin McCrea were members of the band.

New Herrington's new banner going home through Old Elvet. The banner shows the portraits of A.J. Cook, Peter Lee and J.Keir Hardie, with the motto: 'Men of the People.'

Usworth banner coming over Elvet Bridge, homeward bound. It had been the first to arrive in the city at 7.30am. The banner carries a shoulder-length portrait of Keir Hardie.

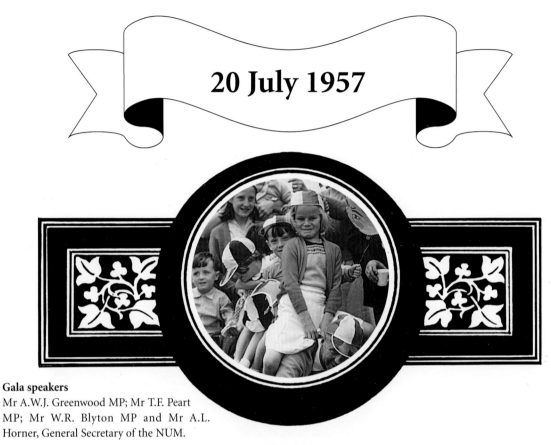

20 July 1957

Gala speakers
Mr A.W.J. Greenwood MP; Mr T.F. Peart MP; Mr W.R. Blyton MP and Mr A.L. Horner, General Secretary of the NUM.

Cathedral service
Preacher: The Rt Revd Dr M.H. Harland, Lord Bishop of Durham.
Easington Colliery Band, bandmaster Mr C. Peacock.
Harton Silver Band, bandmaster Mr George Mather.
Dawdon Colliery Band, bandmaster Mr Stan McDonald.

Mayor: Councillor W.A.H. Shepherd.

Historical Notes
January
Lilley Drift ceased production.

April
Harbour House Drift (near Leamside), ceased production.

June
Mr A. Hesler elected agent for DMA. Membership of Mineworkers' Pension Scheme made compulsory for new entrants into mining industry.

July
Greencroft Tower Colliery, Lanchester, ceased production.

July 20
Gala attendance down due to bus strike.

July
Thrislington Colliery, Cornforth, was Production champion.
The Durham County Brass Band League Championship was won by Easington Colliery.

Dawdon Colliery banner and mascots coming down Gilesgate bank. Like this one, many banners started off from Sherburn Road Ends. To the right is Billy Wood and behind the young boy is Stan McDonald, bandmaster.

Dawdon mascots and followers passing the Royal County Hotel.

Two rows of young dancers swinging along Old Elvet, with Marsden banner in the distance. The balcony of the Waterloo Hotel provides an excellent view.

A Scottish pipe band marches past the balcony, to the admiration of the speakers and guests.

The Rt Revd Dr M.H. Harland, Bishop of Durham – said to be the first bishop to attend the Gala – on the balcony along with other guests and speakers, Sam Watson, Hugh Gaitskell and William Lawther are among the VIPs.

Older spectators outside the Old Elvet shops smile for the camera as the gentleman doffs his bowler hat.

Near the end of Old Elvet a young man gives his girlfriend a lift for the rest of the journey to the racecourse.

The three massed bands (Newbiggin and Lynemouth, South Moor and Wardley) prepare for the playing of *Gresford* in front of the speakers' platform.

Three young band-members from Newbiggin and Lynemouth (see above).

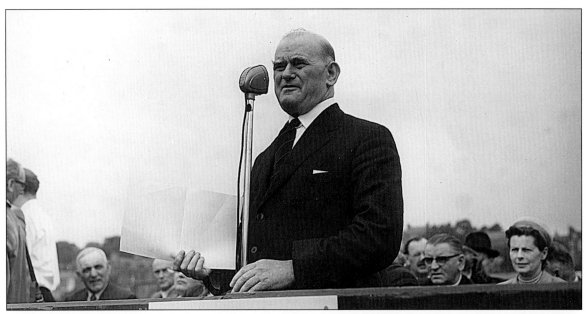

Sam Watson at the microphone. Referring to the bus strike, he said: "There will always be a Durham Miners' Gala even if the buses have no wheels."

'A heavy load.' Jockey caps were the fashionable head-gear this year.

Candy floss time, The two older girls at the rear are said to be Sally and Eleanor Pilkington from Bearpark.

Resting on the step outside the Assize Court door, Old Elvet, after the rain had stopped.

Sheltering from the rain outside the main door of Durham Prison, late afternoon (note the tightly-guarded coconut prizes). *The Durham County Advertiser* reported that the rain came down from 12.30pm to 4.30pm.

Many families came into Durham on foot, Mr Charles Wesley Wild and his wife, Dorothea, and their children, Charles Wesley and James Edward, were photographed walking from Sherburn Village.

Weary visitors make their way to the north-bound platform, Durham Railway Station, for the homeward journey. Due to the bus strike the estimated attendance was 40 per cent down on the previous year.

Sacriston Colliery's new banner, unveiled on the eve of the Gala by Dr Sam Watson (centre). It shows the standing figure of Earl Attlee.

As usual, traffic was banned from Durham for 12 hours. This year, because of the bus strike, more people came to the Gala by their own transport. Special car parks, like this one at Sherburn Road, were full to capacity.

19 July 1958

Gala speakers
The Rt Hon J.H. Wilson MP; the Rt Hon
A.Robens, MP; Miss Alice Bacon MP and Mr A.L. Horner, General Secretary of the NUM.

Cathedral service
Preacher: Canon C.B. Sampson, Vicar of Leeds.

Esh Welfare Band, bandmaster Mr R. White.
Thornley Colliery Band, bandmaster Mr E.G.T. Kitto.
Silksworth Colliery Band, bandmaster Mr J. Peacock.

Mayor: Councillor J.A. Naylor.

Historical Notes
July
Towneley Emma Colliery was Production champion.

August
South Shildon and West Brandon (near Waterhouses) Drifts ceased production.

August
Opening of Fenhall Drift.

November
Princes Street Drift (near Shildon) and Alma Colliery ceased production.

November
Opening of Murton Coking Plant.
The Durham County Brass Band League Championship was won by Crookhall Colliery.

Hedley Hope band and banner at the bottom of Elvet Bridge, photographed from the balcony of the Waterloo Hotel. The banner shows the Good Samaritan.

Clara Vale banner (from the Ryton area) displaying the pattern-book image of 'Labour and Peace'. The shop windows (top) of John Brews and Co Ltd are protected with planks to prevent possible injury.

Officials lead in the banner of Crookhall followed by the band.

Langley Park band and banner, showing an artistic impression of their 'Aim', a tree-lined street with houses and gardens. The portrait inset shows Joseph Robertshaw, Lodge chairman (1924-54). This was added after 1954.

New Shildon banner, displaying the portrait of Dr Hugh Dalton (former MP for Bishop Auckland), enters from New Elvet. Hugh Dalton himself (his raincoat round his shoulders) walks with the officials. The banner of Deaf Hill follows.

Chilton band and banner arriving from New Elvet.

Albert Laskey of Murton entertains with the playing of the bones, near the County Hotel.

Hugh Gaitskell waves to the crowds from the balcony.

Crowds on the slopes welcome the banners in. The attendance this year was estimated at about 200,000.

Almost midday and the banners are still arriving. The one in the foreground is that of Witton Colliery, Sacriston, showing the Hermitage, with the motto: 'And came to be healed of their wounds.'

The speakers and guests arriving on The Racecourse led by Sam Watson, followed by the Mayor, Councillor J.A. Naylor, the Mayoress, Mrs Leslie Oates, Hugh Gaitskell and Mr Martin Jones (Town Clerk).

The Mayor, Councillor J.A. Naylor, addresses the crowd. He said that during the playing of the miners' hymn *Gresford*, he would have liked to have heard the people singing it, if there had been words. Sam Watson replied: "We can't set words to the hymn and we don't intend to." Presumably this was his way of saying that no words could be worthy of such an emotive tune.

Sam Watson introduces Harold Wilson, MP for Huyton.

The audience listens to what Mr Wilson has to say.

The conductor rehearses the massed bands in the playing of *Gresford*, prior to the arrival of the speakers. Three of the bands taking part are Crookhall, Langley Park and Murton.

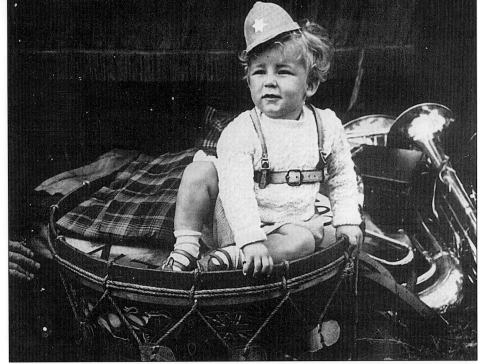

Left in charge of the instruments.

Two young 'Red Indians' larking around with their bow and arrows.

Ryhope band and banner going home over Elvet Bridge. The scene depicted shows a miner, his family and three servicemen above the words: 'Unity-In-Peace-In War.'

South Pelaw banner, showing the pictures of Peter Lee and A.J. Cook.

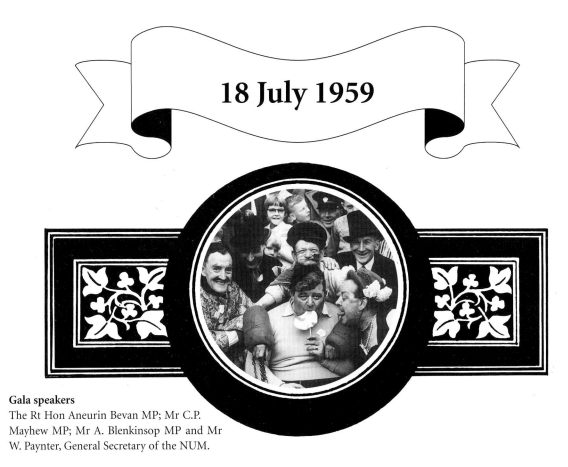

18 July 1959

Gala speakers
The Rt Hon Aneurin Bevan MP; Mr C.P.
Mayhew MP; Mr A. Blenkinsop MP and Mr
W. Paynter, General Secretary of the NUM.

Cathedral service
Preacher: The Rt Revd Mervyn Armstrong, Bishop of Jarrow.
Craghead Colliery Band, bandmaster Mr W.E. Cunningham.
The Boldon Colliery Workmens' Band, bandmaster Mr H. Hurst.
Chopwell Colliery Band, bandmaster Mr H. Wright.

Mayor: Sir James Duff.

Historical Notes
January
Closure of Ouston 'E' and East Hedley Hope Collieries.

February
Castle Eden Colliery ceased production.

July
Handen Hold Colliery was Production champion.

September
Opening of Hawthorn Combined Mine.

October 8
Harold MacMillan returns the Tories to power, using the slogan: 'You've never had it so good!'

October
Ramshaw Colliery ceased production.
The Durham County Brass Band League Championship was won by Horden Colliery.

Speakers and guests on the balcony of the Royal County Hotel greet the early arrivals. On the right are Hugh Gaitskell and Aneurin Bevan (Shadow Foreign Secretary).

The Shakespeare band passing the Dunelm Hotel, led by the bandmaster Mr R. Clark. On the left is John Mollon from Sherburn Road.

Thrislington banner
(showing Conishead
Priory) led by a Scottish
pipe band along Old Elvet.

A mounted escort keeps an eye on the lines of dancers as they take control of this stretch of the road, on their way to the racecourse.

The Chief Constable Alex Muir (in shirt-sleeve order) watches the processions march on to The Racecourse. The large wall is that of Durham Prison.

Young girls in their fashionable dresses lead a banner showing Conishead Priory.

Dawdon Jolly Boys ahead of their banner. Left to right are Joe Walker, Sam Hughes, Billy Wood, Tom Gills, Tom Buris (sic) and not known.

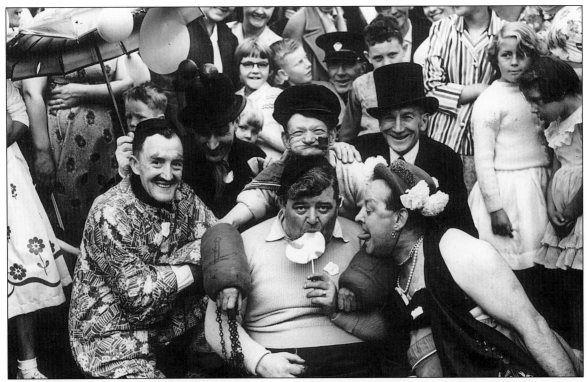

The Dawdon Jolly Boys reach their final destination (see p216-17).

Young folk swing their way on to the field.

A linked row of smiling girls and boys ahead of the band and banner of Wheatley Hill.

The arrival of the Mayor, Sir James Duff, followed by Aneurin Bevan. In later years the presence of the police was more noticeable.

Sir James Duff gives a civic welcome to those attending, watched by Sam Watson and (seated) Aneurin Bevan.

The Racecourse showing crowds around the speakers platform. The building and landscaped gardens of Bede College occupy the land on the other side of the river.

Bowburn's new banner, centre, which had been unfurled on the eve of the Gala by Christopher Mayhew MP. Jack Ramshaw of Bowburn is in the light trousers. It shows a distant view of The Racecourse from Pelaw Wood.

Dancers going home ahead of Fishburn's new banner. The building on the left, part of the Dunelm Hotel.

A farewell wave from the balcony to the crowds as they leave for home.

A tattooed mascot said to be Lenny Cumiskey from Brandon, ahead of his procession. Some names attached are Steve Cutting, Jerry Berry, Harold Mitchell and Fred Donaldson from Seaham.

4.45pm. The band plays as Washington Glebe banner makes its way home, over Elvet Bridge.

4.50pm. Marley Hill banner and followers make their way home.

16 July 1960

Gala speakers
Mr F.E. Noel-Baker MP; Mr F.T. Willey MP; Mr
C.F. Grey MP; J.H. Whitney, American Ambassador and Mr W. Paynter, General Secretary of the NUM.

Cathedral service
Preacher: The Rt Revd L.S. Hunter, Bishop of Sheffield.

Brandon Colliery Band, bandmaster Mr G. Brown.
Hetton Silver Prize Band, bandmaster Mr G. Scorer (with Eppleton banner).
Durham Shakespeare Band, bandmaster Mr R.A. Clark (with Bradley Shops Mechanics' banner).

Mayor: Councillor J.W. Bell.

Historical Notes
February.
South Garesfield Colliery ceased production.

July.
Garesfield Colliery ceased production.

July.
Silksworth Colliery was Production champion.

August
Ushaw Moor Colliery ceased production.
The Durham County Brass Band League Championship was won by Easington Colliery.

Marching to the Gala for the last time, Ushaw Moor banner halts outside the County Hospital gates to greet an old friend, Mr Ike Finlay, who had been specially wheeled out by a nurse.

A bunch of bright young girls, with the early morning sun on their faces, dance forward ahead of a banner near the County Hospital.

Officials lead Washington 'F' Pit banner, followed by the band.

The 3rd (751) American Air Force band was led by Sgt Borden Brown of Cleveland, Ohio, marches in front of Tanfield Lea banner on Elvet Bridge. It was the first overseas band to take part in the Gala, bringing with it a more modern style of music.

A close up view of Tanfield Lea banner and followers. It shows a female charioteer with four charging horses (see p227). Behind it is South Moor No.1 banner.

New Shildon banner bearing the portrait of Dr Hugh Dalton MP, who is walking in front with the officials.

West Auckland banner, bearing the portrait of Arthur Horner, passing the Dunelm Hotel. Note the arched entrance and sign of Chapel Passage on the left.

Fishburn officials take pride in the bringing in of their banner.

Peter Lee's great-granddaughter, Carol, with her mother (right), Winifred Coleman. They always followed Wheatley Hill banner which bore the portrait of their ancestor.

Durham and Chester-le-Street Red Cross
members outside Shire Hall, Old Elvet.

The bandmaster leads Burnhope band and banner, showing Durham Cathedral. Three of the four boys on the left are carrying their fathers' instrument cases.

Middridge Drift banner showing Sir Stafford Cripps, Lord Lawson of Beamish and Ernest Bevin, enters The Racecourse.

Easington's new banner, purchased in 1959, bearing likenesses of Keir Hardie and Robert Smillie. This repeated the design of the former banner.

Chopwell banner, called 'the Red Banner' because of the portraits of Marx and Lenin on it.

Wheatley Hill followers behind their banner which bears the portrait of Peter Lee.

The arrival of Pelton Fell banner and its followers.

A good photograph showing the gathering shortly before midday. On the far right is the banner of Harraton Colliery followed by its band. Near the centre of the picture, two mounted policemen mingle with the crowd.

The four massed bands play Gresford.

The Mayor, Alderman J.W. Bell, welcoming the speakers and guests. Behind the platform are the banners (left to right) of Thornley, Roddymoor, Mainsforth and Brandon. The American Ambassador, Mr J.H. Whitney, and his wife, were guests this year. At the bottom of the picture the newspaper reporters are busy taking notes.

Mr Sam Watson, in his opening words, paid a moving tribute to the late Mr Aneurin Bevan, who had spoken at seven Galas.

Bradley Shops banner (Leadgate), Palace Green. It shows a carpenter's shop, with Jesus and Joseph, entitled: 'The perfect craftsman'.

A vicar from Brandon and Mr G. Brown, bandmaster, lead the colliery band of Brandon towards the main door of the Cathedral.

Drinkers outside the Court Inn, Court Lane. Many of the pubs raised their prices, beer sold at 1s 1d a pint on Friday shot up to 1s 5d on Saturday. Bottled beer, such as brown ale, was cheerfully being bought at 2s 6d a bottle. The quality of some of the draught beer was such that the connoisseur preferred to pay extra for bottles.

The USAF band, almost lost in the throng, was the centre of attraction this year.

Crowds in Old Elvet spot the camera on the Royal County Hotel balcony. The estimated attendance this year was 250,000.

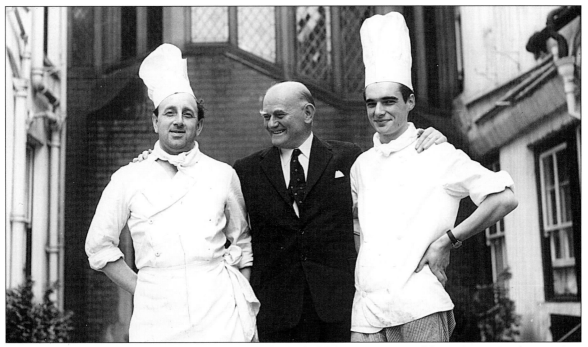

Sam Watson congratulating the Royal County Hotel chefs who had fed over 300 guests of the Durham Miners' Association. They are head chef Bill Nicholson (left) and second chef Tim Denham (right).

INDEX